HOW TO DRAW MONSTERS

HOW TO DRAW GODZILLA

Derrick Richards

Enslow PUBLISHING

Please visit our website, www.enslow.com. For a free color catalog of all our high-quality books,
call toll free 1-800-398-2504 or fax 1-877-980-4454

Published in 2027 by
Enslow Publishing
2544 Clinton Street
Buffalo, NY 14224

Portions of this work were originally authored by Greg Roza and published as *Drawing Movie Monsters Step-by-Step: Drawing Godzilla*. All new material in this edition is authored by Derrick Richards.

Cataloging-in-Publication Data
Names: Richards, Derrick.
Title: How to draw Godzilla / Derrick Richards.
Description: Buffalo, NY : Enslow Publishing, 2027. | Series: How to draw monsters | Includes glossary and index.
Identifiers: ISBN 9781978548725 (pbk.) | ISBN 9781978548732 (library bound) | ISBN 9781978548749 (ebook)
Subjects: LCSH: Godzilla (Fictitious character)--Juvenile literature. | Monsters in art--Juvenile literature. | Drawing--Technique--Juvenile literature.
Classification: LCC NC825.M6 R534 2027 | DDC 743.87--dc23

Printed in China

Photos Credits: Cover, p. 1 Satoshi Mizushima/Shutterstock.com; cover, p. 1 Shutterstock AI Generator/Shutterstock.com; cover, p. 1, 5, 7, 9, 11, 13, 15, 17, 19, 21 (notebook) Liena10/Shutterstock.com; p. 5 (ruler) karen roach/Shutterstock.com; p. 5 (colored pencils) Avocado_studio/Shutterstock.com; p. 5 (marker) New Africa/Shutterstock.com; p. 6, 8, 12, 16 Wikipedia/Wikipedia; p. 10 zepkatana/Shutterstock.com; p. 14 Public Domain; p. 20 Fandom/Wikipedia; p. 22 Phoenix Pixels/Shutterstock.com

CPSIA compliance information: Batch #QSENS27: For further information, contact Enslow Publishing, New York, New York, at 1-800-398-2504.

CONTENTS

EVERYBODY RUN!

You look out over the sea from the coast of Japan. What's that rumbling under the surface?

Suddenly, a giant dinosaur rises from the water. It stomps toward land—and toward you. Cars are crushed. Buildings fall. Everybody run! It's Godzilla!

Godzilla is a fictional monster that first appeared in a Japanese movie in 1954. Since then, it has become an international **icon.**

Godzilla caused fear wherever it went. But in many movies, it often helped save the world from other giant monsters. Good or bad, Godzilla has become one of the most memorable movie monsters of all time.

Godzilla's style may have changed over time, but it's always fun to draw. Let's learn how!

You will need the following supplies:

PAPER

PENCIL

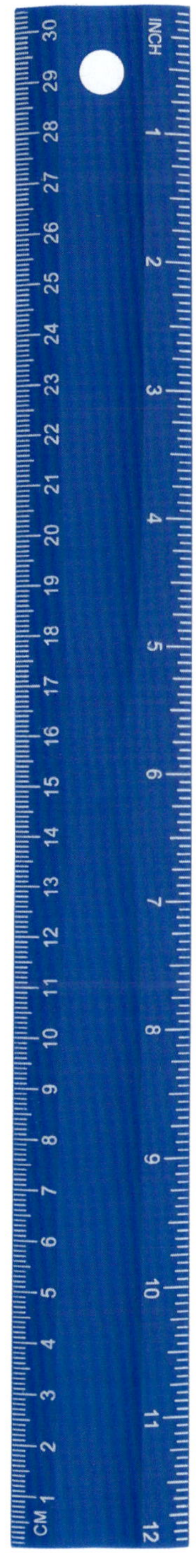

RULER

MARKER

COLORED PENCILS

GODZILLA IS BORN

Japanese filmmakers originally named the now-famous movie monster Gojira. The name "Gojira" came from a mashup of two Japanese words: *gorira*, which means "gorilla," and *kujira*, which means "whale." English speakers changed the monster's name to Godzilla.

The first Godzilla movie was **released** in 1954. It was called *Gojira*. The movie begins with reports of ships sinking at sea. Later, Godzilla destroys a city. The monster breathes fire, smashes bridges, and breaks power lines. In the end, only a new **weapon** can stop it.

Let's start by drawing Godzilla as it attacks a military base.

At the time of its release, *Gojira* was the most expensive Japanese film ever made.

Step 1

Draw two shapes for the head and the outline of the body.

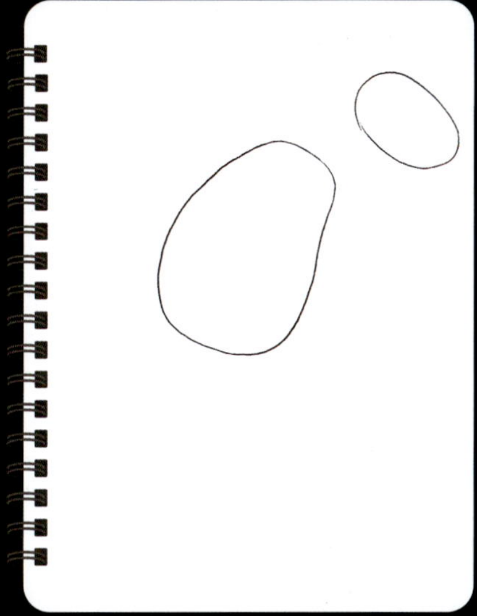

Step 2

Add a cluster of small circles and ovals around the body.

Step 3

Draw lines to join the head to the body. Draw the shoulders and arms by joining the top ovals. Join the lower ovals to make the legs and the tail.

Step 4

Add the mouth outline. Draw hands and feet.

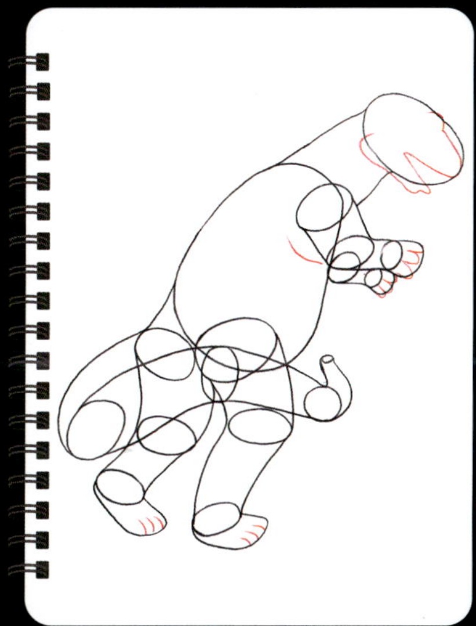

Step 5

Add eyes, claws, scales, a nostril, and the plates on Godzilla's back. Erase the small circles and ovals.

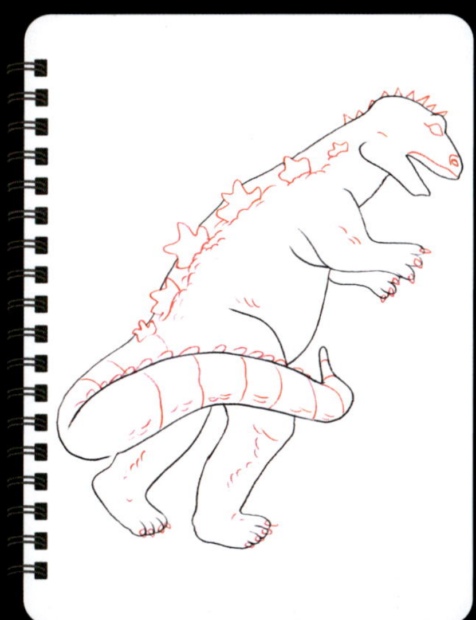

Step 6

Add details and color your drawing.

GODZILLA, KING OF THE MONSTERS

Gojira was popular in Japan at the time of its release. In 1956, American filmmakers bought *Gojira* from Japanese filmmakers. The American filmmakers cut out much of the original film. They filmed new scenes with a Canadian actor. This actor played a reporter covering the Godzilla story. These new scenes helped explain the movie's action without having to re-record the Japanese actors' voices.

The American filmmakers renamed the movie *Godzilla, King of the Monsters!* The American movie helped make Godzilla popular all over the world. Let's draw this scene from *Gojira*, where Godzilla is stomping through a government building in Tokyo.

Godzilla is known for smashing through cities, including any buildings that got in its way.

Step 1

Draw an oval for the head. Draw the outline of the body.

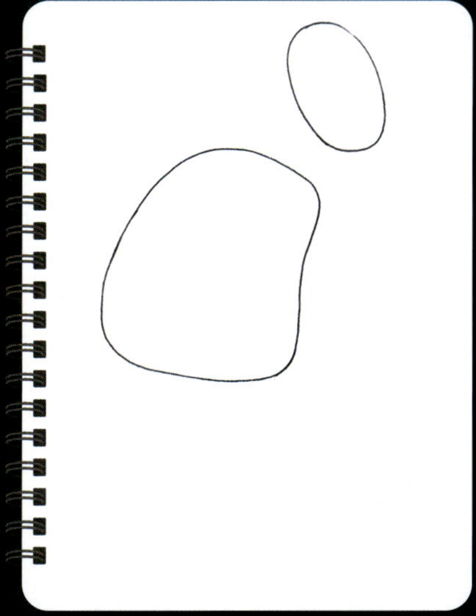

Step 2

Add three small ovals on the top left corner of the body outline.

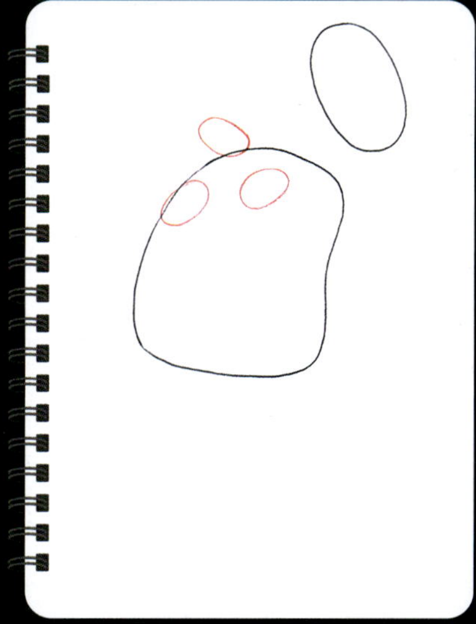

Step 3

Join the small ovals to make the right arm. Add Godzilla's left arm and the outline of the building in the background.

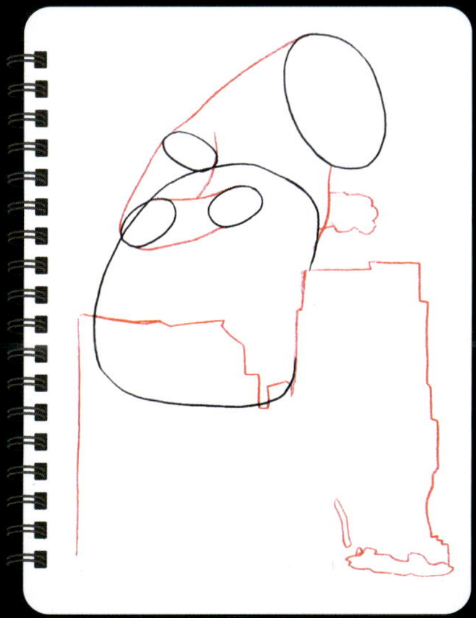

Step 4

Add details to the buildings. Draw details on Godzilla's face and hands.

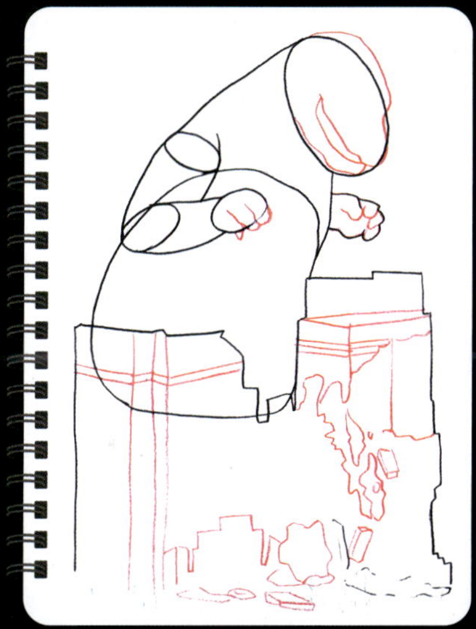

Step 5

Add the eyes, nose, scales, and claws. Draw the plates along the monster's back. Erase extra lines.

Step 6

Add details to Godzilla's face and body. Add the windows and the final details to the building. Add color.

A TRUE TERROR

How did the films bring the monster to life? Godzilla was played by an actor wearing a rubber suit. Sometimes the actor had to be lifted by wires to make it look like Godzilla was flying. Filmmakers built **miniature** cities for Godzilla to smash. These tiny cities made Godzilla look like it was hundreds of feet tall!

With today's special effects, some people may not find the original Godzilla scary. But in the 1950s, people thought the monster was realistic and terrifying!

Step 1

Draw an oval.

Step 2

Add a smaller circle below the oval.

Step 3

Join the circle and the oval. Add smaller ovals on top of the bigger oval and a guide line for the head.

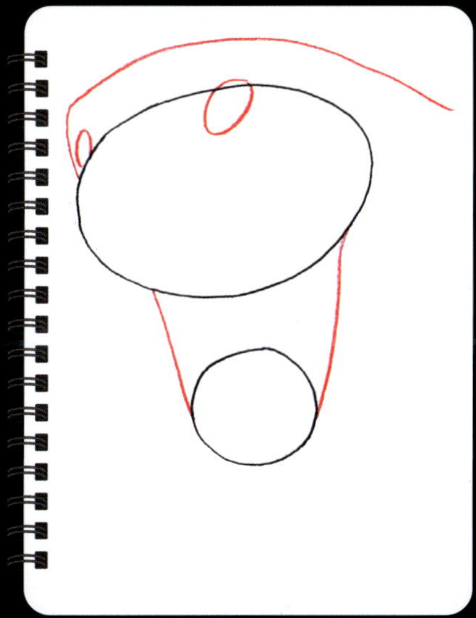

Step 4

Add lines for the eyes and the mouth.

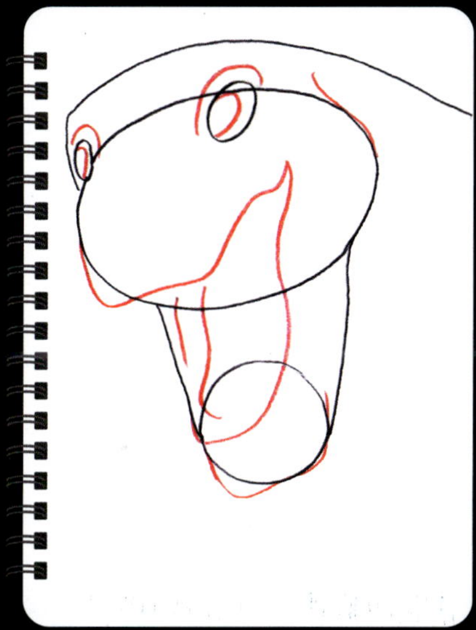

Step 5

Add details to the eyes. Draw Godzilla's nostrils, teeth, and the plates on top of its head. Erase guide shapes.

Step 6

Add scales on the face and complete the facial features.

MONSTER VS. MONSTER

Godzilla continued to change over the years, as many more *Gojira* films were released. In some movies, Godzilla is the hero that saves the people of Japan. Godzilla is often shown battling other giant monsters.

Godzilla has even fought other famous movie monsters. In 1962, it faced off against King Kong in the movie *King Kong vs. Godzilla*. These two giant monsters have proven to be a popular matchup. Four more movies have been made featuring King Kong and Godzilla! Most recently, the two faced off in 2024's *Godzilla x Kong: The New Empire*.

Now, let's try drawing Godzilla from the 1966 movie *Godzilla vs. the Sea Monster*.

In different movies, Godzilla has battled a moth, a shrimp, a three-headed dragon, and even a robot Godzilla!

Step 1

Draw a small oval for the head. Add a shape for the body outline.

Step 2

Add small circles and ovals all around the body outline.

Step 3

Join the circles and ovals to create arms, legs, hands, feet, and tail.

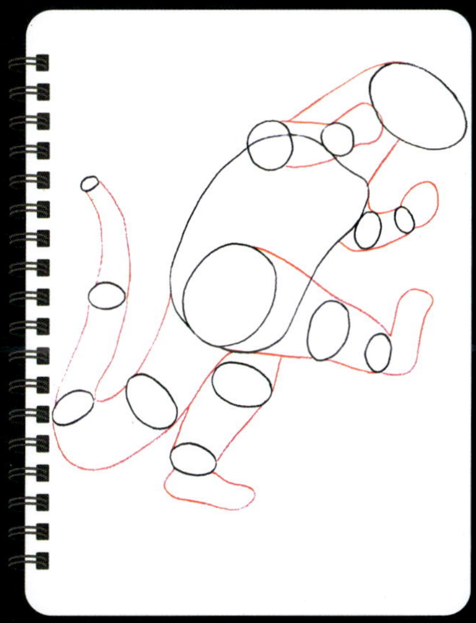

Step 4

Draw the mouth, hands, feet, and chest.

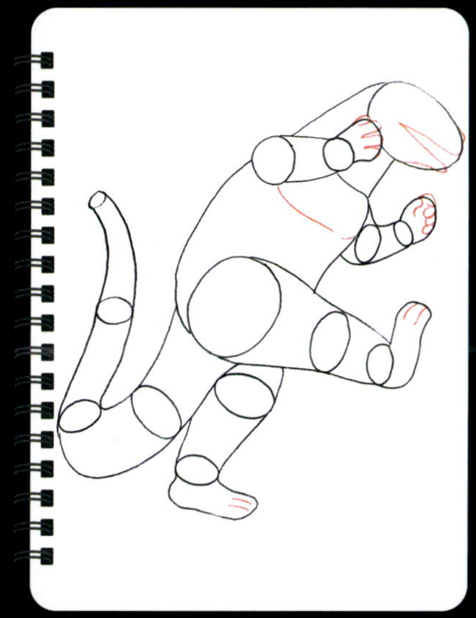

Step 5

Add the eyes, claws, spikes, and scales. Erase the guides.

Step 6

Add Godzilla's teeth. Add details to its body and fire shooting out of its mouth.

GODZILLA COMES TO NEW YORK!

Godzilla is a 1998 American remake of the original. It was the twenty-third film in the **franchise** and the first American version.

In this film, Godzilla stomps through New York, terrorizing many famous sites and buildings in the city. The military tries to find a way to kill the monster. It fights with all its weapons, but bullets, rockets, and missiles don't cause any harm. Godzilla takes down three helicopters with its fiery breath.

Let's try drawing this scary shot from the 1998 movie!

The 1998 *Godzilla* movie was supposed to be the first in a trilogy, but the sequels were canceled.

Step 1

Draw a circular shape for the head. Add the body outline.

Step 2

Add small circles and ovals around the body.

Step 3

Connect the ovals and circles to make the arms, legs, hands, feet, and tail.

Step 4

Draw an outline around the face. Add lines to the hands and feet.

Step 5

Add Godzilla's eyes, nose, mouth, chest, claws, and scales. Erase the guide shapes.

Step 6

Add scales and final details to the face.

SPECIAL EFFECTS

Unlike earlier Godzilla movies, the filmmakers used computers to create the monster and other **special effects** in *Godzilla*. This allowed the filmmakers to show Godzilla destroying famous New York City buildings. The computer special effects looked more "real" to audiences than the rubber suit and miniature city **techniques** of the older movies.

Let's try drawing Godzilla as it fights off tanks!

These tanks were no match for the mighty Godzilla!

Step 1

Draw an oval for the face. Add a rounded shape for the body outline.

Step 2

Add circles and ovals around the body.

Step 3

Join the ovals and circles to create the shoulders, arms, legs, hands, feet, and tail.

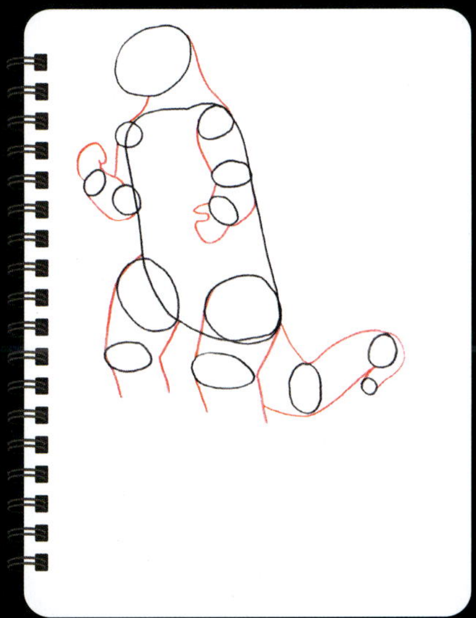

Step 4

Add Godzilla's eyes, nostrils, mouth, chest, and claws.

Step 5

Add details to the face, chest, and hands. Erase the guides.

Step 6

Finish your drawing by adding details and color.

BATTLING SPACE ALIENS

Godzilla continues to fascinate audiences. Both Japanese and American filmmakers have made several new Godzilla movies since the first American movie was released in 1998. Many of Godzilla's old enemies also showed up in these movies.

In 2004, Japanese filmmakers released *Godzilla: Final Wars*. In this film, space **aliens** attack Earth by releasing giant monsters. It's up to Godzilla to save the planet. This is Godzilla's toughest battle yet!

Now, let's draw Godzilla standing tall.

This 2004 film celebrated 50 years of Godzilla movies! It was the twenty-eighth film in the franchise.

Step 1

Draw an oval for the face. Add a rounded shape for the body outline.

Step 2

Add circles and ovals around the body.

Step 3

Join the circles and ovals to create the shoulders, arms, hands, legs, feet, and tail.

Step 4

Add Godzilla's eyes, nostrils, mouth, chest, and claws.

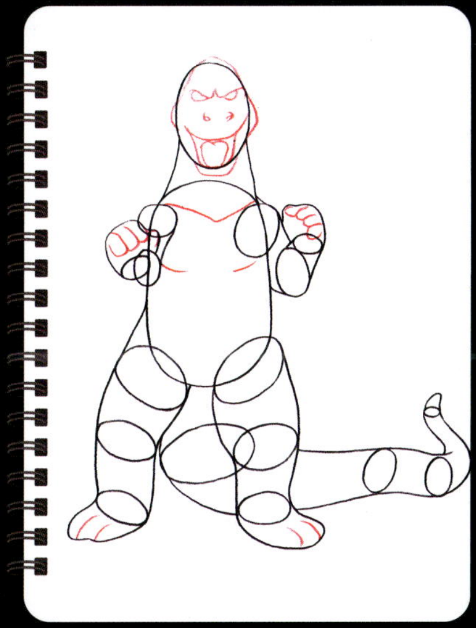

Step 5

Add details to the face, chest, and hands. Erase the guides.

Step 6

Finish your drawing by adding details and color.

GODZILLA LIVES ON

Over the past 70 years, Godzilla has starred in nearly 40 films. This movie monster has had quite a **career**. Godzilla is not just a movie star. The world's most popular monster also appears in comics, cartoons, video games, and television shows. You can even find Godzilla toys.

Godzilla is a hard monster to kill. Fans today still watch the old Godzilla movies. Many eagerly await Godzilla's next adventure.

Now, let's draw this memorable picture of the monster eating a train from the movie that started it all, *Gojira*.

For nearly 70 years, Godzilla has proven to be unstoppable!

Step 1

Draw a round shape for the head. Add the outline of the body.

Step 2

Add small ovals and circles around and below the body.

Step 3

Add lines to connect the ovals and circles. This will finish Godzilla's basic outline.

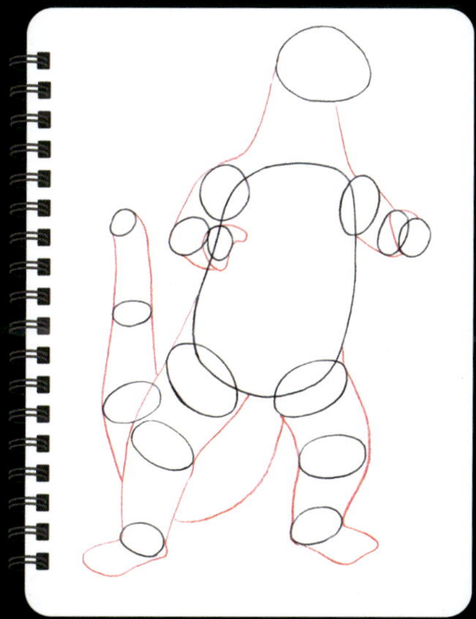

Step 4

Draw the claws, fingers, and chest. Add rectangles for the train. Draw the tip of the tail and the toes.

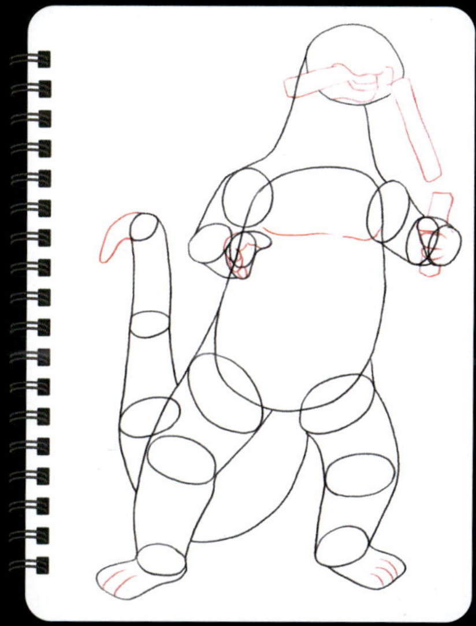

Step 5

Add the eyes and scales. Draw details on the train. Add the spikes on Godzilla's head. Erase the guide shapes.

Step 6

Add final details to the face and body.

DID YOU KNOW?

In 1997, a real dinosaur, *Gojirasaurus*, was named after the movie monster.

The original monster suit used in *Gojira* (1954) weighed more than 200 pounds (91 kg). The actor could only walk about 30 feet (9.1 m) at a time.

The original version of *Gojira* was not released in the United States until 2004.

No one really knows for sure if Godzilla is male or female.

Godzilla's son was introduced to fans in the 1967 movie *The Son of Godzilla*.

Godzilla has a star on the famous Hollywood Walk of Fame!

GLOSSARY

alien (AY-lee-un) A creature from outer space.

career (kuh-REER) A job.

franchise (FRAN-chize) A collection of related films that all share the same universe.

icon (EYE-kahn) Something that is widely admired for having influence.

miniature (MIH-nee-uh-chur) A small copy of something larger.

released (ree-LEEST) To make something available to the public.

special effects (SPEH-shul uh-FEKTS) Tricks in moviemaking that make scenes that are fake look real.

techniques (tek-NEEKS) A way of doing something.

weapon (WEH-pun) Objects used to hurt or kill.

INDEX

ON THE INTERNET

All Godzilla Movies in Order

www.fandango.com/movie-news/all-godzilla-movies-in-order-ordered-by-release-date-754984

Check out this list of all 38 Godzilla movies so far. See how this giant monster has evolved over the years!

Godzilla

https://godzilla.com/

Discover all things Godzilla, from games to collectibles and more!